# This
# Budget Planner
# belongs to:

goal
_____

$30,000
Down
Payment

gaby

I'm one step away
from being rich ...

All I need now
is money

# Monthly Budget

## Income

| | |
|---|---|
| Income 1 | |
| Income 2 | |
| Other Income | |
| Total Income | |

## Expenses

Month

Budget

| Bill to be paid | Date due | Amount | Paid | Notes |
|---|---|---|---|---|
| | | | | |
| | | | | |
| | | | | |
| | | | | |
| | | | | |
| | | | | |
| | | | | |
| | | | | |
| | | | | |
| | | | | |
| | | | | |

# Other expenses

| other Expenses | Date | Amount | Paid | Notes |
|---|---|---|---|---|
|  |  |  |  |  |
|  |  |  |  |  |
|  |  |  |  |  |
|  |  |  |  |  |
|  |  |  |  |  |
|  |  |  |  |  |
|  |  |  |  |  |
|  |  |  |  |  |
|  |  |  |  |  |
|  |  |  |  |  |
| Total |  |  |  |  |

Notes:

_____

_____

_____

_____

_____

# Weekly Expense Tracker

## Monday   Date ___ /___ /___

| Description | Amount |
|---|---|
|  |  |
|  |  |
|  |  |
|  |  |
|  |  |
|  |  |
| Total |  |

## Tuesday   Date ___ /___ /___

| Description | Amount |
|---|---|
|  |  |
|  |  |
|  |  |
|  |  |
|  |  |
|  |  |
| Total |  |

## Wednesday   Date ___ /___ /___

| Description | Amount |
|---|---|
|  |  |
|  |  |
|  |  |
|  |  |
|  |  |
|  |  |
| Total |  |

## Thursday   Date ___ /___ /___

| Description | Amount |
|---|---|
|  |  |
|  |  |
|  |  |
|  |  |
|  |  |
| Total |  |

Budget:

Brought forward:

# Weekly Expense Tracker

## Friday    Date ___ /___ /___

| Description | Amount |
|---|---|
|  |  |
|  |  |
|  |  |
|  |  |
|  |  |
|  |  |
| Total |  |

## Saturday    Date ___ /___ /___

| Description | Amount |
|---|---|
|  |  |
|  |  |
|  |  |
|  |  |
|  |  |
|  |  |
| Total |  |

## Sunday    Date ___ /___ /___

| Description | Amount |
|---|---|
|  |  |
|  |  |
|  |  |
|  |  |
|  |  |
|  |  |
| Total |  |

## Notes

|  |
|---|
|  |
|  |
|  |
|  |
|  |
|  |
|  |

Budget:

Brought forward:

# Weekly Expense Tracker

## Monday     Date ___ /___ /___

| Description | Amount |
|---|---|
|  |  |
|  |  |
|  |  |
|  |  |
|  |  |
| Total |  |

## Tuesday     Date ___ /___ /___

| Description | Amount |
|---|---|
|  |  |
|  |  |
|  |  |
|  |  |
|  |  |
| Total |  |

## Wednesday     Date ___ /___ /___

| Description | Amount |
|---|---|
|  |  |
|  |  |
|  |  |
|  |  |
|  |  |
| Total |  |

## Thursday     Date ___ /___ /___

| Description | Amount |
|---|---|
|  |  |
|  |  |
|  |  |
|  |  |
|  |  |
| Total |  |

Budget:

Brought forward:

# Weekly Expense Tracker

## Friday  Date ___ /___ /___

| Description | Amount |
|---|---|
|  |  |
|  |  |
|  |  |
|  |  |
|  |  |
|  |  |
| Total |  |

## Saturday  Date ___ /___ /___

| Description | Amount |
|---|---|
|  |  |
|  |  |
|  |  |
|  |  |
|  |  |
|  |  |
| Total |  |

## Sunday  Date ___ /___ /___

| Description | Amount |
|---|---|
|  |  |
|  |  |
|  |  |
|  |  |
|  |  |
|  |  |
| Total |  |

## Notes

Budget:

Brought forward:

# Weekly Expense Tracker

## Monday  Date ___ /___ /___

| Description | Amount |
|---|---|
|  |  |
|  |  |
|  |  |
|  |  |
|  |  |
|  |  |
| Total |  |

## Tuesday  Date ___ /___ /___

| Description | Amount |
|---|---|
|  |  |
|  |  |
|  |  |
|  |  |
|  |  |
|  |  |
| Total |  |

## Wednesday Date ___ /___ /___

| Description | Amount |
|---|---|
|  |  |
|  |  |
|  |  |
|  |  |
|  |  |
|  |  |
| Total |  |

## Thursday Date ___ /___ /___

| Description | Amount |
|---|---|
|  |  |
|  |  |
|  |  |
|  |  |
|  |  |
| Total |  |

Budget:

Brought forward:

# Weekly Expense Tracker

## Friday    Date ___ /___ /___

| Description | Amount |
|---|---|
| | |
| | |
| | |
| | |
| | |
| | |
| Total | |

## Saturday    Date ___ /___ /___

| Description | Amount |
|---|---|
| | |
| | |
| | |
| | |
| | |
| | |
| Total | |

## Sunday Date ___ /___ /___

| Description | Amount |
|---|---|
| | |
| | |
| | |
| | |
| | |
| | |
| Total | |

## Notes

| |
|---|
| |
| |
| |
| |
| |
| |

Budget:

Brought forward:

# Weekly Expense Tracker

## Monday  Date ___ /___ /___

| Description | Amount |
|---|---|
|  |  |
|  |  |
|  |  |
|  |  |
|  |  |
| Total |  |

## Tuesday  Date ___ /___ /___

| Description | Amount |
|---|---|
|  |  |
|  |  |
|  |  |
|  |  |
|  |  |
| Total |  |

## Wednesday  Date ___ /___ /___

| Description | Amount |
|---|---|
|  |  |
|  |  |
|  |  |
|  |  |
|  |  |
| Total |  |

## Thursday  Date ___ /___ /___

| Description | Amount |
|---|---|
|  |  |
|  |  |
|  |  |
|  |  |
|  |  |
| Total |  |

Budget:

Brought forward:

# Weekly Expense Tracker

## Friday     Date ___ /___ /___

| Description | Amount |
|---|---|
|  |  |
|  |  |
|  |  |
|  |  |
|  |  |
|  |  |
| Total |  |

## Saturday     Date ___ /___ /___

| Description | Amount |
|---|---|
|  |  |
|  |  |
|  |  |
|  |  |
|  |  |
|  |  |
| Total |  |

## Sunday Date ___ /___ /___

| Description | Amount |
|---|---|
|  |  |
|  |  |
|  |  |
|  |  |
|  |  |
| Total |  |

## Notes

|  |
|---|
|  |
|  |
|  |
|  |
|  |
|  |

Budget:

Brought forward:

# Weekly Expense Tracker

## Monday    Date ___ /___ /___

| Description | Amount |
|---|---|
|  |  |
|  |  |
|  |  |
|  |  |
|  |  |
|  |  |
| Total |  |

## Tuesday    Date ___ /___ /___

| Description | Amount |
|---|---|
|  |  |
|  |  |
|  |  |
|  |  |
|  |  |
|  |  |
| Total |  |

## Wednesday    Date ___ /___ /___

| Description | Amount |
|---|---|
|  |  |
|  |  |
|  |  |
|  |  |
|  |  |
|  |  |
| Total |  |

## Thursday    Date ___ /___ /___

| Description | Amount |
|---|---|
|  |  |
|  |  |
|  |  |
|  |  |
|  |  |
| Total |  |

Budget:

Brought forward:

# Weekly Expense Tracker

## Friday  Date ___ /___ /___

| Description | Amount |
|---|---|
|  |  |
|  |  |
|  |  |
|  |  |
|  |  |
| Total |  |

## Saturday  Date ___ /___ /___

| Description | Amount |
|---|---|
|  |  |
|  |  |
|  |  |
|  |  |
|  |  |
| Total |  |

## Sunday Date ___ /___ /___

| Description | Amount |
|---|---|
|  |  |
|  |  |
|  |  |
|  |  |
|  |  |
| Total |  |

## Notes

| |
|---|
|  |
|  |
|  |
|  |
|  |
|  |
|  |

Budget:

Brought forward:

# Monthly Budget

## Income

| | |
|---|---|
| Income 1 | |
| Income 2 | |
| Other Income | |
| Total Income | |

## Expenses

Month

Budget

| Bill to be paid | Date due | Amount | Paid | Notes |
|---|---|---|---|---|
| | | | | |
| | | | | |
| | | | | |
| | | | | |
| | | | | |
| | | | | |
| | | | | |
| | | | | |
| | | | | |
| | | | | |
| | | | | |
| | | | | |

# Other expenses

| other Expenses | Date | Amount | Paid | Notes |
|---|---|---|---|---|
| | | | | |
| | | | | |
| | | | | |
| | | | | |
| | | | | |
| | | | | |
| | | | | |
| | | | | |
| | | | | |
| | | | | |
| Total | | | | |

Notes:

_____

_____

_____

_____

_____

# Weekly Expense Tracker

## Monday  Date ___ /___ /___

| Description | Amount |
|---|---|
| | |
| | |
| | |
| | |
| | |
| | |
| Total | |

## Tuesday  Date ___ /___ /___

| Description | Amount |
|---|---|
| | |
| | |
| | |
| | |
| | |
| | |
| Total | |

## Wednesday Date ___ /___ /___

| Description | Amount |
|---|---|
| | |
| | |
| | |
| | |
| | |
| | |
| Total | |

## Thursday Date ___ /___ /___

| Description | Amount |
|---|---|
| | |
| | |
| | |
| | |
| | |
| Total | |

Budget:

Brought forward:

# Weekly Expense Tracker

## Friday    Date ___ /___ /___

| Description | Amount |
|---|---|
|  |  |
|  |  |
|  |  |
|  |  |
|  |  |
|  |  |
| Total |  |

## Saturday    Date ___ /___ /___

| Description | Amount |
|---|---|
|  |  |
|  |  |
|  |  |
|  |  |
|  |  |
|  |  |
| Total |  |

## Sunday   Date ___ /___ /___

| Description | Amount |
|---|---|
|  |  |
|  |  |
|  |  |
|  |  |
|  |  |
| Total |  |

## Notes

Budget:

Brought forward:

# Weekly Expense Tracker

## Monday    Date ___ /___ /___

| Description | Amount |
|---|---|
| | |
| | |
| | |
| | |
| | |
| | |
| Total | |

## Tuesday    Date ___ /___ /___

| Description | Amount |
|---|---|
| | |
| | |
| | |
| | |
| | |
| | |
| Total | |

## Wednesday    Date ___ /___ /___

| Description | Amount |
|---|---|
| | |
| | |
| | |
| | |
| | |
| Total | |

## Thursday    Date ___ /___ /___

| Description | Amount |
|---|---|
| | |
| | |
| | |
| | |
| | |
| Total | |

Budget:

Brought forward:

# Weekly Expense Tracker

## Friday    Date ___ /___ /___

| Description | Amount |
|---|---|
|  |  |
|  |  |
|  |  |
|  |  |
|  |  |
|  |  |
| Total |  |

## Saturday    Date ___ /___ /___

| Description | Amount |
|---|---|
|  |  |
|  |  |
|  |  |
|  |  |
|  |  |
|  |  |
| Total |  |

## Sunday Date ___ /___ /___

| Description | Amount |
|---|---|
|  |  |
|  |  |
|  |  |
|  |  |
|  |  |
| Total |  |

## Notes

|  |
|---|
|  |
|  |
|  |
|  |
|  |
|  |

Budget:

Brought forward:

# Weekly Expense Tracker

## Monday    Date ___ /___ /___

| Description | Amount |
|---|---|
|  |  |
|  |  |
|  |  |
|  |  |
|  |  |
|  |  |
| Total |  |

## Tuesday    Date ___ /___ /___

| Description | Amount |
|---|---|
|  |  |
|  |  |
|  |  |
|  |  |
|  |  |
|  |  |
| Total |  |

## Wednesday  Date ___ /___ /___

| Description | Amount |
|---|---|
|  |  |
|  |  |
|  |  |
|  |  |
|  |  |
|  |  |
| Total |  |

## Thursday  Date ___ /___ /___

| Description | Amount |
|---|---|
|  |  |
|  |  |
|  |  |
|  |  |
|  |  |
| Total |  |

Budget:

Brought forward:

# Weekly Expense Tracker

## Friday    Date ___ /___ /___

| Description | Amount |
|---|---|
|  |  |
|  |  |
|  |  |
|  |  |
|  |  |
|  |  |
| Total |  |

## Saturday    Date ___ /___ /___

| Description | Amount |
|---|---|
|  |  |
|  |  |
|  |  |
|  |  |
|  |  |
|  |  |
| Total |  |

## Sunday Date ___ /___ /___

| Description | Amount |
|---|---|
|  |  |
|  |  |
|  |  |
|  |  |
|  |  |
|  |  |
| Total |  |

## Notes

Budget:                    Brought forward:

# Weekly Expense Tracker

## Monday  Date ___ /___ /___

| Description | Amount |
|---|---|
|  |  |
|  |  |
|  |  |
|  |  |
|  |  |
|  |  |
| Total |  |

## Tuesday  Date ___ /___ /___

| Description | Amount |
|---|---|
|  |  |
|  |  |
|  |  |
|  |  |
|  |  |
|  |  |
| Total |  |

## Wednesday  Date ___ /___ /___

| Description | Amount |
|---|---|
|  |  |
|  |  |
|  |  |
|  |  |
|  |  |
|  |  |
| Total |  |

## Thursday  Date ___ /___ /___

| Description | Amount |
|---|---|
|  |  |
|  |  |
|  |  |
|  |  |
|  |  |
| Total |  |

Budget:

Brought forward:

# Weekly Expense Tracker

## Friday    Date ___ /___ /___

| Description | Amount |
|---|---|
|  |  |
|  |  |
|  |  |
|  |  |
|  |  |
| Total |  |

## Saturday    Date ___ /___ /___

| Description | Amount |
|---|---|
|  |  |
|  |  |
|  |  |
|  |  |
|  |  |
| Total |  |

## Sunday    Date ___ /___ /___

| Description | Amount |
|---|---|
|  |  |
|  |  |
|  |  |
|  |  |
|  |  |
| Total |  |

## Notes

Budget:

Brought Forward:

# Weekly Expense Tracker

## Monday    Date ___ /___ /___

| Description | Amount |
|---|---|
|  |  |
|  |  |
|  |  |
|  |  |
|  |  |
|  |  |
| Total |  |

## Tuesday    Date ___ /___ /___

| Description | Amount |
|---|---|
|  |  |
|  |  |
|  |  |
|  |  |
|  |  |
|  |  |
| Total |  |

## Wednesday    Date ___ /___ /___

| Description | Amount |
|---|---|
|  |  |
|  |  |
|  |  |
|  |  |
|  |  |
|  |  |
| Total |  |

## Thursday    Date ___ /___ /___

| Description | Amount |
|---|---|
|  |  |
|  |  |
|  |  |
|  |  |
|  |  |
| Total |  |

Budget:

Brought forward:

# Weekly Expense Tracker

## Friday     Date ___ /___ /___

| Description | Amount |
|---|---|
| | |
| | |
| | |
| | |
| | |
| Total | |

## Saturday     Date ___ /___ /___

| Description | Amount |
|---|---|
| | |
| | |
| | |
| | |
| | |
| Total | |

## Sunday Date ___ /___ /___

| Description | Amount |
|---|---|
| | |
| | |
| | |
| | |
| | |
| Total | |

## Notes

Budget:                          Brought forward:

# Monthly Budget

## Income

| | |
|---|---|
| Income 1 | |
| Income 2 | |
| Other Income | |
| Total Income | |

## Expenses

Month

Budget

| Bill to be paid | Date due | Amount | Paid | Notes |
|---|---|---|---|---|
| | | | | |
| | | | | |
| | | | | |
| | | | | |
| | | | | |
| | | | | |
| | | | | |
| | | | | |
| | | | | |
| | | | | |
| | | | | |
| | | | | |

# Other expenses

| Other Expenses | Date | Amount | Paid | Notes |
|---|---|---|---|---|
| | | | | |
| | | | | |
| | | | | |
| | | | | |
| | | | | |
| | | | | |
| | | | | |
| | | | | |
| | | | | |
| | | | | |
| Total | | | | |

## Notes:
_____

_____

_____

_____

_____

# Weekly Expense Tracker

## Monday Date ___ /___ /___

| Description | Amount |
|---|---|
|  |  |
|  |  |
|  |  |
|  |  |
|  |  |
| Total |  |

## Tuesday Date ___ /___ /___

| Description | Amount |
|---|---|
|  |  |
|  |  |
|  |  |
|  |  |
|  |  |
| Total |  |

## Wednesday Date ___ /___ /___

| Description | Amount |
|---|---|
|  |  |
|  |  |
|  |  |
|  |  |
|  |  |
| Total |  |

## Thursday Date ___ /___ /___

| Description | Amount |
|---|---|
|  |  |
|  |  |
|  |  |
|  |  |
|  |  |
| Total |  |

Budget:

Brought forward:

# Weekly Expense Tracker

## Friday    Date ___ /___ /___

| Description | Amount |
|---|---|
|  |  |
|  |  |
|  |  |
|  |  |
|  |  |
| Total |  |

## Saturday    Date ___ /___ /___

| Description | Amount |
|---|---|
|  |  |
|  |  |
|  |  |
|  |  |
|  |  |
| Total |  |

## Sunday Date ___ /___ /___

| Description | Amount |
|---|---|
|  |  |
|  |  |
|  |  |
|  |  |
|  |  |
| Total |  |

## Notes

|  |
|---|
|  |
|  |
|  |
|  |
|  |
|  |

Budget:

Brought forward:

# Weekly Expense Tracker

## Monday  Date ___ /___ /___

| Description | Amount |
|---|---|
|  |  |
|  |  |
|  |  |
|  |  |
|  |  |
|  |  |
| Total |  |

## Tuesday  Date ___ /___ /___

| Description | Amount |
|---|---|
|  |  |
|  |  |
|  |  |
|  |  |
|  |  |
|  |  |
| Total |  |

## Wednesday  Date ___ /___ /___

| Description | Amount |
|---|---|
|  |  |
|  |  |
|  |  |
|  |  |
|  |  |
|  |  |
| Total |  |

## Thursday  Date ___ /___ /___

| Description | Amount |
|---|---|
|  |  |
|  |  |
|  |  |
|  |  |
|  |  |
| Total |  |

Budget:

Brought forward:

# Weekly Expense Tracker

## Friday    Date ___ /___ /___

| Description | Amount |
|---|---|
| | |
| | |
| | |
| | |
| | |
| Total | |

## Saturday    Date ___ /___ /___

| Description | Amount |
|---|---|
| | |
| | |
| | |
| | |
| | |
| Total | |

## Sunday Date ___ /___ /___

| Description | Amount |
|---|---|
| | |
| | |
| | |
| | |
| | |
| Total | |

## Notes

| |
|---|
| |
| |
| |
| |
| |

Budget:

Brought forward:

# Weekly Expense Tracker

## Monday　Date ___ /___ /___

| Description | Amount |
|---|---|
|  |  |
|  |  |
|  |  |
|  |  |
|  |  |
| Total |  |

## Tuesday　Date ___ /___ /___

| Description | Amount |
|---|---|
|  |  |
|  |  |
|  |  |
|  |  |
|  |  |
| Total |  |

## Wednesday Date ___ /___ /___

| Description | Amount |
|---|---|
|  |  |
|  |  |
|  |  |
|  |  |
|  |  |
| Total |  |

## Thursday Date ___ /___ /___

| Description | Amount |
|---|---|
|  |  |
|  |  |
|  |  |
|  |  |
| Total |  |

Budget:

Brought forward:

# Weekly Expense Tracker

## Friday    Date ___ /___ /___

| Description | Amount |
|---|---|
|  |  |
|  |  |
|  |  |
|  |  |
|  |  |
| Total |  |

## Saturday    Date ___ /___ /___

| Description | Amount |
|---|---|
|  |  |
|  |  |
|  |  |
|  |  |
| Total |  |

## Sunday Date ___ /___ /___

| Description | Amount |
|---|---|
|  |  |
|  |  |
|  |  |
|  |  |
|  |  |
| Total |  |

## Notes

Budget:

Brought forward:

# Weekly Expense Tracker

## Monday   Date ___ /___ /___

| Description | Amount |
|-------------|--------|
|             |        |
|             |        |
|             |        |
|             |        |
|             |        |
|             |        |
| Total       |        |

## Tuesday   Date ___ /___ /___

| Description | Amount |
|-------------|--------|
|             |        |
|             |        |
|             |        |
|             |        |
|             |        |
|             |        |
| Total       |        |

## Wednesday   Date ___ /___ /___

| Description | Amount |
|-------------|--------|
|             |        |
|             |        |
|             |        |
|             |        |
|             |        |
|             |        |
| Total       |        |

## Thursday   Date ___ /___ /___

| Description | Amount |
|-------------|--------|
|             |        |
|             |        |
|             |        |
|             |        |
|             |        |
|             |        |
| Total       |        |

Budget:

Brought forward:

# Weekly Expense Tracker

## Friday    Date ___ /___ /___

| Description | Amount |
|---|---|
|  |  |
|  |  |
|  |  |
|  |  |
|  |  |
| Total |  |

## Saturday    Date ___ /___ /___

| Description | Amount |
|---|---|
|  |  |
|  |  |
|  |  |
|  |  |
|  |  |
| Total |  |

## Sunday Date ___ /___ /___

| Description | Amount |
|---|---|
|  |  |
|  |  |
|  |  |
|  |  |
|  |  |
| Total |  |

## Notes

|  |
|---|
|  |
|  |
|  |
|  |
|  |
|  |

Budget:

Brought forward:

# Weekly Expense Tracker

## Monday  Date ___ /___ /___

| Description | Amount |
|---|---|
|  |  |
|  |  |
|  |  |
|  |  |
|  |  |
|  |  |
| Total |  |

## Tuesday  Date ___ /___ /___

| Description | Amount |
|---|---|
|  |  |
|  |  |
|  |  |
|  |  |
|  |  |
|  |  |
| Total |  |

## Wednesday  Date ___ /___ /___

| Description | Amount |
|---|---|
|  |  |
|  |  |
|  |  |
|  |  |
|  |  |
|  |  |
| Total |  |

## Thursday  Date ___ /___ /___

| Description | Amount |
|---|---|
|  |  |
|  |  |
|  |  |
|  |  |
|  |  |
| Total |  |

Budget:

Brought forward:

# Weekly Expense Tracker

## Friday     Date ___ /___ /___

| Description | Amount |
|---|---|
|  |  |
|  |  |
|  |  |
|  |  |
|  |  |
|  |  |
| Total |  |

## Saturday     Date ___ /___ /___

| Description | Amount |
|---|---|
|  |  |
|  |  |
|  |  |
|  |  |
|  |  |
|  |  |
| Total |  |

## Sunday     Date ___ /___ /___

| Description | Amount |
|---|---|
|  |  |
|  |  |
|  |  |
|  |  |
|  |  |
|  |  |
| Total |  |

## Notes

Budget:                              Brought forward:

# Monthly Budget

## Income

| | |
|---|---|
| Income 1 | |
| Income 2 | |
| Other Income | |
| Total Income | |

## Expenses

Month

Budget

| Bill to be paid | Date due | Amount | Paid | Notes |
|---|---|---|---|---|
| | | | | |
| | | | | |
| | | | | |
| | | | | |
| | | | | |
| | | | | |
| | | | | |
| | | | | |
| | | | | |
| | | | | |
| | | | | |
| | | | | |

# Other expenses

| Other Expenses | Date | Amount | Paid | Notes |
|---|---|---|---|---|
|  |  |  |  |  |
|  |  |  |  |  |
|  |  |  |  |  |
|  |  |  |  |  |
|  |  |  |  |  |
|  |  |  |  |  |
|  |  |  |  |  |
|  |  |  |  |  |
|  |  |  |  |  |
|  |  |  |  |  |
| Total |  |  |  |  |

Notes:

_____

_____

_____

_____

_____

# Weekly Expense Tracker

## Monday  Date ___ /___ /___

| Description | Amount |
|---|---|
| | |
| | |
| | |
| | |
| | |
| | |
| Total | |

## Tuesday  Date ___ /___ /___

| Description | Amount |
|---|---|
| | |
| | |
| | |
| | |
| | |
| | |
| Total | |

## Wednesday Date ___ /___ /___

| Description | Amount |
|---|---|
| | |
| | |
| | |
| | |
| | |
| | |
| Total | |

## Thursday Date ___ /___ /___

| Description | Amount |
|---|---|
| | |
| | |
| | |
| | |
| | |
| Total | |

Budget:

Brought forward:

# Weekly Expense Tracker

## Friday  Date ___ / ___ / ___

| Description | Amount |
|---|---|
|  |  |
|  |  |
|  |  |
|  |  |
|  |  |
|  |  |
| Total |  |

## Saturday  Date ___ / ___ / ___

| Description | Amount |
|---|---|
|  |  |
|  |  |
|  |  |
|  |  |
|  |  |
|  |  |
| Total |  |

## Sunday  Date ___ / ___ / ___

| Description | Amount |
|---|---|
|  |  |
|  |  |
|  |  |
|  |  |
|  |  |
| Total |  |

## Notes

|  |
|---|
|  |
|  |
|  |
|  |
|  |
|  |

Budget:

Brought forward:

# Weekly Expense Tracker

## Monday    Date ___ /___ /___

| Description | Amount |
|---|---|
| | |
| | |
| | |
| | |
| | |
| | |
| Total | |

## Tuesday    Date ___ /___ /___

| Description | Amount |
|---|---|
| | |
| | |
| | |
| | |
| | |
| | |
| Total | |

## Wednesday Date ___ /___ /___

| Description | Amount |
|---|---|
| | |
| | |
| | |
| | |
| | |
| | |
| Total | |

## Thursday Date ___ /___ /___

| Description | Amount |
|---|---|
| | |
| | |
| | |
| | |
| | |
| Total | |

Budget:

Brought forward:

# Weekly Expense Tracker

## Friday    Date ___ /___ /___

| Description | Amount |
|-------------|--------|
|             |        |
|             |        |
|             |        |
|             |        |
|             |        |
|             |        |
| Total       |        |

## Saturday    Date ___ /___ /___

| Description | Amount |
|-------------|--------|
|             |        |
|             |        |
|             |        |
|             |        |
|             |        |
|             |        |
| Total       |        |

## Sunday    Date ___ /___ /___

| Description | Amount |
|-------------|--------|
|             |        |
|             |        |
|             |        |
|             |        |
|             |        |
| Total       |        |

## Notes

Budget:

Brought forward:

# Weekly Expense Tracker

## Monday    Date ___ /___ /___

| Description | Amount |
|---|---|
| | |
| | |
| | |
| | |
| | |
| | |
| Total | |

## Tuesday    Date ___ /___ /___

| Description | Amount |
|---|---|
| | |
| | |
| | |
| | |
| | |
| | |
| Total | |

## Wednesday Date ___ /___ /___

| Description | Amount |
|---|---|
| | |
| | |
| | |
| | |
| | |
| | |
| Total | |

## Thursday Date ___ /___ /___

| Description | Amount |
|---|---|
| | |
| | |
| | |
| | |
| | |
| Total | |

Budget:

Brought forward:

# Weekly Expense Tracker

## Friday   Date ___ /___ /___

| Description | Amount |
|---|---|
|  |  |
|  |  |
|  |  |
|  |  |
|  |  |
|  |  |
| Total |  |

## Saturday   Date ___ /___ /___

| Description | Amount |
|---|---|
|  |  |
|  |  |
|  |  |
|  |  |
|  |  |
|  |  |
| Total |  |

## Sunday   Date ___ /___ /___

| Description | Amount |
|---|---|
|  |  |
|  |  |
|  |  |
|  |  |
|  |  |
|  |  |
| Total |  |

## Notes

|  |
|---|
|  |
|  |
|  |
|  |
|  |
|  |

Budget:

Brought forward:

# Weekly Expense Tracker

## Monday  Date ___ / ___ / ___

| Description | Amount |
|---|---|
|  |  |
|  |  |
|  |  |
|  |  |
|  |  |
| Total |  |

## Tuesday  Date ___ / ___ / ___

| Description | Amount |
|---|---|
|  |  |
|  |  |
|  |  |
|  |  |
|  |  |
| Total |  |

## Wednesday  Date ___ / ___ / ___

| Description | Amount |
|---|---|
|  |  |
|  |  |
|  |  |
|  |  |
|  |  |
| Total |  |

## Thursday  Date ___ / ___ / ___

| Description | Amount |
|---|---|
|  |  |
|  |  |
|  |  |
|  |  |
|  |  |
| Total |  |

Budget:

Brought forward:

# Weekly Expense Tracker

## Friday  Date ___ /___ /___

| Description | Amount |
|---|---|
|  |  |
|  |  |
|  |  |
|  |  |
|  |  |
| Total |  |

## Saturday  Date ___ /___ /___

| Description | Amount |
|---|---|
|  |  |
|  |  |
|  |  |
|  |  |
|  |  |
| Total |  |

## Sunday  Date ___ /___ /___

| Description | Amount |
|---|---|
|  |  |
|  |  |
|  |  |
|  |  |
|  |  |
| Total |  |

## Notes

|  |
|---|
|  |
|  |
|  |
|  |
|  |
|  |

Budget:

Brought forward:

# Weekly Expense Tracker

## Monday    Date ___ /___ /___

| Description | Amount |
|---|---|
|  |  |
|  |  |
|  |  |
|  |  |
|  |  |
|  |  |
| Total |  |

## Tuesday    Date ___ /___ /___

| Description | Amount |
|---|---|
|  |  |
|  |  |
|  |  |
|  |  |
|  |  |
|  |  |
| Total |  |

## Wednesday Date ___ /___ /___

| Description | Amount |
|---|---|
|  |  |
|  |  |
|  |  |
|  |  |
|  |  |
|  |  |
| Total |  |

## Thursday Date ___ /___ /___

| Description | Amount |
|---|---|
|  |  |
|  |  |
|  |  |
|  |  |
|  |  |
| Total |  |

Budget:

Brought forward:

# Weekly Expense Tracker

## Friday    Date ___ /___ /___

| Description | Amount |
|-------------|--------|
|             |        |
|             |        |
|             |        |
|             |        |
|             |        |
| Total       |        |

## Saturday    Date ___ /___ /___

| Description | Amount |
|-------------|--------|
|             |        |
|             |        |
|             |        |
|             |        |
|             |        |
| Total       |        |

## Sunday    Date ___ /___ /___

| Description | Amount |
|-------------|--------|
|             |        |
|             |        |
|             |        |
|             |        |
|             |        |
| Total       |        |

## Notes

Budget:

Brought forward:

# Monthly Budget

## Income

| | |
|---|---|
| Income 1 | |
| Income 2 | |
| Other Income | |
| Total Income | |

## Expenses

Month

Budget

| Bill to be paid | Date due | Amount | Paid | Notes |
|---|---|---|---|---|
| | | | | |
| | | | | |
| | | | | |
| | | | | |
| | | | | |
| | | | | |
| | | | | |
| | | | | |
| | | | | |
| | | | | |
| | | | | |
| | | | | |

# Other expenses

| Other Expenses | Date | Amount | Paid | Notes |
|---|---|---|---|---|
|  |  |  |  |  |
|  |  |  |  |  |
|  |  |  |  |  |
|  |  |  |  |  |
|  |  |  |  |  |
|  |  |  |  |  |
|  |  |  |  |  |
|  |  |  |  |  |
|  |  |  |  |  |
|  |  |  |  |  |
| Total |  |  |  |  |

*Notes:*

_____

_____

_____

_____

_____

# Weekly Expense Tracker

## Monday    Date ___ /___ /___

| Description | Amount |
|---|---|
|  |  |
|  |  |
|  |  |
|  |  |
|  |  |
| Total |  |

## Tuesday    Date ___ /___ /___

| Description | Amount |
|---|---|
|  |  |
|  |  |
|  |  |
|  |  |
|  |  |
| Total |  |

## Wednesday Date ___ /___ /___

| Description | Amount |
|---|---|
|  |  |
|  |  |
|  |  |
|  |  |
|  |  |
| Total |  |

## Thursday Date ___ /___ /___

| Description | Amount |
|---|---|
|  |  |
|  |  |
|  |  |
|  |  |
| Total |  |

Budget:

Brought forward:

# Weekly Expense Tracker

## Friday    Date ___ /___ /___

| Description | Amount |
|---|---|
|  |  |
|  |  |
|  |  |
|  |  |
|  |  |
| Total |  |

## Saturday    Date ___ /___ /___

| Description | Amount |
|---|---|
|  |  |
|  |  |
|  |  |
|  |  |
|  |  |
| Total |  |

## Sunday  Date ___ /___ /___

| Description | Amount |
|---|---|
|  |  |
|  |  |
|  |  |
|  |  |
|  |  |
| Total |  |

## Notes

|  |
|---|
|  |
|  |
|  |
|  |
|  |
|  |

Budget:

Brought forward:

# Weekly Expense Tracker

## Monday    Date ___ / ___ / ___

| Description | Amount |
|---|---|
|  |  |
|  |  |
|  |  |
|  |  |
|  |  |
|  |  |
| Total |  |

## Tuesday    Date ___ / ___ / ___

| Description | Amount |
|---|---|
|  |  |
|  |  |
|  |  |
|  |  |
|  |  |
|  |  |
| Total |  |

## Wednesday  Date ___ / ___ / ___

| Description | Amount |
|---|---|
|  |  |
|  |  |
|  |  |
|  |  |
|  |  |
|  |  |
| Total |  |

## Thursday  Date ___ / ___ / ___

| Description | Amount |
|---|---|
|  |  |
|  |  |
|  |  |
|  |  |
|  |  |
|  |  |
| Total |  |

Budget:

Brought forward:

# Weekly Expense Tracker

## Friday    Date ___ /___ /___

| Description | Amount |
|---|---|
|  |  |
|  |  |
|  |  |
|  |  |
|  |  |
| Total |  |

## Saturday    Date ___ /___ /___

| Description | Amount |
|---|---|
|  |  |
|  |  |
|  |  |
|  |  |
|  |  |
| Total |  |

## Sunday    Date ___ /___ /___

| Description | Amount |
|---|---|
|  |  |
|  |  |
|  |  |
|  |  |
|  |  |
| Total |  |

## Notes

Budget:

Brought forward:

# Weekly Expense Tracker

## Monday    Date ___ /___ /___

| Description | Amount |
|---|---|
|  |  |
|  |  |
|  |  |
|  |  |
|  |  |
| Total |  |

## Tuesday    Date ___ /___ /___

| Description | Amount |
|---|---|
|  |  |
|  |  |
|  |  |
|  |  |
|  |  |
| Total |  |

## Wednesday Date ___ /___ /___

| Description | Amount |
|---|---|
|  |  |
|  |  |
|  |  |
|  |  |
|  |  |
| Total |  |

## Thursday Date ___ /___ /___

| Description | Amount |
|---|---|
|  |  |
|  |  |
|  |  |
|  |  |
|  |  |
| Total |  |

Budget:

Brought forward:

# Weekly Expense Tracker

## Friday    Date ___ /___ /___

| Description | Amount |
|-------------|--------|
|             |        |
|             |        |
|             |        |
|             |        |
|             |        |
| Total       |        |

## Saturday    Date ___ /___ /___

| Description | Amount |
|-------------|--------|
|             |        |
|             |        |
|             |        |
|             |        |
|             |        |
| Total       |        |

## Sunday  Date ___ /___ /___

| Description | Amount |
|-------------|--------|
|             |        |
|             |        |
|             |        |
|             |        |
|             |        |
| Total       |        |

## Notes

|   |
|---|
|   |
|   |
|   |
|   |
|   |

Budget:

Brought forward:

# Weekly Expense Tracker

## Monday  Date ___ /___ /___

| Description | Amount |
|---|---|
|  |  |
|  |  |
|  |  |
|  |  |
|  |  |
|  |  |
| Total |  |

## Tuesday  Date ___ /___ /___

| Description | Amount |
|---|---|
|  |  |
|  |  |
|  |  |
|  |  |
|  |  |
|  |  |
| Total |  |

## Wednesday Date ___ /___ /___

| Description | Amount |
|---|---|
|  |  |
|  |  |
|  |  |
|  |  |
|  |  |
|  |  |
| Total |  |

## Thursday Date ___ /___ /___

| Description | Amount |
|---|---|
|  |  |
|  |  |
|  |  |
|  |  |
|  |  |
|  |  |
| Total |  |

Budget:

Brought forward:

# Weekly Expense Tracker

## Friday     Date ___ /___ /___

| Description | Amount |
|---|---|
|  |  |
|  |  |
|  |  |
|  |  |
|  |  |
|  |  |
| Total |  |

## Saturday     Date ___ /___ /___

| Description | Amount |
|---|---|
|  |  |
|  |  |
|  |  |
|  |  |
|  |  |
|  |  |
| Total |  |

## Sunday     Date ___ /___ /___

| Description | Amount |
|---|---|
|  |  |
|  |  |
|  |  |
|  |  |
|  |  |
|  |  |
| Total |  |

## Notes

Budget:

Brought forward:

# Weekly Expense Tracker

## Monday  Date ___ /___ /___

| Description | Amount |
|---|---|
|  |  |
|  |  |
|  |  |
|  |  |
|  |  |
|  |  |
| Total |  |

## Tuesday  Date ___ /___ /___

| Description | Amount |
|---|---|
|  |  |
|  |  |
|  |  |
|  |  |
|  |  |
|  |  |
| Total |  |

## Wednesday Date ___ /___ /___

| Description | Amount |
|---|---|
|  |  |
|  |  |
|  |  |
|  |  |
|  |  |
|  |  |
| Total |  |

## Thursday Date ___ /___ /___

| Description | Amount |
|---|---|
|  |  |
|  |  |
|  |  |
|  |  |
|  |  |
| Total |  |

Budget:

Brought forward:

# Weekly Expense Tracker

## Friday    Date ___ /___ /___

| Description | Amount |
|-------------|--------|
|             |        |
|             |        |
|             |        |
|             |        |
|             |        |
|             |        |
| Total       |        |

## Saturday    Date ___ /___ /___

| Description | Amount |
|-------------|--------|
|             |        |
|             |        |
|             |        |
|             |        |
|             |        |
|             |        |
| Total       |        |

## Sunday    Date ___ /___ /___

| Description | Amount |
|-------------|--------|
|             |        |
|             |        |
|             |        |
|             |        |
|             |        |
|             |        |
| Total       |        |

## Notes

Budget:

Brought forward:

# Monthly Budget

## Income

| | |
|---|---|
| Income 1 | |
| Income 2 | |
| Other Income | |
| Total Income | |

## Expenses

Month

Budget

| Bill to be paid | Date due | Amount | Paid | Notes |
|---|---|---|---|---|
| | | | | |
| | | | | |
| | | | | |
| | | | | |
| | | | | |
| | | | | |
| | | | | |
| | | | | |
| | | | | |
| | | | | |
| | | | | |
| | | | | |

# Other expenses

| Other Expenses | Date | Amount | Paid | Notes |
|---|---|---|---|---|
| | | | | |
| | | | | |
| | | | | |
| | | | | |
| | | | | |
| | | | | |
| | | | | |
| | | | | |
| | | | | |
| | | | | |
| | | | | |
| Total | | | | |

## Notes:

_____

_____

_____

_____

_____

# Weekly Expense Tracker

## Monday    Date ___ /___ /___

| Description | Amount |
|---|---|
|  |  |
|  |  |
|  |  |
|  |  |
|  |  |
| Total |  |

## Tuesday    Date ___ /___ /___

| Description | Amount |
|---|---|
|  |  |
|  |  |
|  |  |
|  |  |
|  |  |
| Total |  |

## Wednesday Date ___ /___ /___

| Description | Amount |
|---|---|
|  |  |
|  |  |
|  |  |
|  |  |
|  |  |
| Total |  |

## Thursday Date ___ /___ /___

| Description | Amount |
|---|---|
|  |  |
|  |  |
|  |  |
|  |  |
| Total |  |

Budget:

Brought forward:

# Weekly Expense Tracker

## Friday    Date ___ /___ /___

| Description | Amount |
|-------------|--------|
|             |        |
|             |        |
|             |        |
|             |        |
|             |        |
|             |        |
| Total       |        |

## Saturday    Date ___ /___ /___

| Description | Amount |
|-------------|--------|
|             |        |
|             |        |
|             |        |
|             |        |
|             |        |
|             |        |
| Total       |        |

## Sunday Date ___ /___ /___

| Description | Amount |
|-------------|--------|
|             |        |
|             |        |
|             |        |
|             |        |
|             |        |
| Total       |        |

## Notes

|  |
|--|
|  |
|  |
|  |
|  |
|  |

Budget:

Brought forward:

# Weekly Expense Tracker

## Monday    Date ___ / ___ / ___

| Description | Amount |
|---|---|
|  |  |
|  |  |
|  |  |
|  |  |
|  |  |
| Total |  |

## Tuesday    Date ___ / ___ / ___

| Description | Amount |
|---|---|
|  |  |
|  |  |
|  |  |
|  |  |
|  |  |
| Total |  |

## Wednesday    Date ___ / ___ / ___

| Description | Amount |
|---|---|
|  |  |
|  |  |
|  |  |
|  |  |
|  |  |
| Total |  |

## Thursday    Date ___ / ___ / ___

| Description | Amount |
|---|---|
|  |  |
|  |  |
|  |  |
|  |  |
|  |  |
| Total |  |

Budget:

Brought forward:

# Weekly Expense Tracker

## Friday        Date ___ /___ /___

| Description | Amount |
|---|---|
|  |  |
|  |  |
|  |  |
|  |  |
|  |  |
|  |  |
| Total |  |

## Saturday        Date ___ /___ /___

| Description | Amount |
|---|---|
|  |  |
|  |  |
|  |  |
|  |  |
|  |  |
|  |  |
| Total |  |

## Sunday        Date ___ /___ /___

| Description | Amount |
|---|---|
|  |  |
|  |  |
|  |  |
|  |  |
|  |  |
| Total |  |

## Notes

|  |
|---|
|  |
|  |
|  |
|  |
|  |
|  |

Budget:

Brought forward:

# Weekly Expense Tracker

## Monday    Date ___ /___ /___

| Description | Amount |
|---|---|
|  |  |
|  |  |
|  |  |
|  |  |
|  |  |
|  |  |
| Total |  |

## Tuesday    Date ___ /___ /___

| Description | Amount |
|---|---|
|  |  |
|  |  |
|  |  |
|  |  |
|  |  |
|  |  |
| Total |  |

## Wednesday Date ___ /___ /___

| Description | Amount |
|---|---|
|  |  |
|  |  |
|  |  |
|  |  |
|  |  |
|  |  |
| Total |  |

## Thursday Date ___ /___ /___

| Description | Amount |
|---|---|
|  |  |
|  |  |
|  |  |
|  |  |
|  |  |
| Total |  |

Budget:

Brought forward:

# Weekly Expense Tracker

## Friday    Date ___ /___ /___

| Description | Amount |
|---|---|
|  |  |
|  |  |
|  |  |
|  |  |
|  |  |
|  |  |
| Total |  |

## Saturday    Date ___ /___ /___

| Description | Amount |
|---|---|
|  |  |
|  |  |
|  |  |
|  |  |
|  |  |
|  |  |
| Total |  |

## Sunday    Date ___ /___ /___

| Description | Amount |
|---|---|
|  |  |
|  |  |
|  |  |
|  |  |
|  |  |
|  |  |
| Total |  |

## Notes

Budget:

Brought forward:

# Weekly Expense Tracker

## Monday    Date ___ / ___ / ___

| Description | Amount |
|---|---|
| | |
| | |
| | |
| | |
| | |
| | |
| Total | |

## Tuesday    Date ___ / ___ / ___

| Description | Amount |
|---|---|
| | |
| | |
| | |
| | |
| | |
| | |
| Total | |

## Wednesday Date ___ / ___ / ___

| Description | Amount |
|---|---|
| | |
| | |
| | |
| | |
| | |
| | |
| Total | |

## Thursday Date ___ / ___ / ___

| Description | Amount |
|---|---|
| | |
| | |
| | |
| | |
| | |
| | |
| Total | |

Budget:

Brought forward:

# Weekly Expense Tracker

## Friday    Date ___ /___ /___

| Description | Amount |
|---|---|
|  |  |
|  |  |
|  |  |
|  |  |
|  |  |
|  |  |
| Total |  |

## Saturday    Date ___ /___ /___

| Description | Amount |
|---|---|
|  |  |
|  |  |
|  |  |
|  |  |
|  |  |
|  |  |
| Total |  |

## Sunday    Date ___ /___ /___

| Description | Amount |
|---|---|
|  |  |
|  |  |
|  |  |
|  |  |
|  |  |
|  |  |
| Total |  |

## Notes

|  |
|---|
|  |
|  |
|  |
|  |
|  |
|  |

Budget:

Brought forward:

# Weekly Expense Tracker

## Monday    Date ___ /___ /___

| Description | Amount |
|---|---|
|  |  |
|  |  |
|  |  |
|  |  |
|  |  |
| Total |  |

## Tuesday    Date ___ /___ /___

| Description | Amount |
|---|---|
|  |  |
|  |  |
|  |  |
|  |  |
|  |  |
| Total |  |

## Wednesday Date ___ /___ /___

| Description | Amount |
|---|---|
|  |  |
|  |  |
|  |  |
|  |  |
|  |  |
| Total |  |

## Thursday Date ___ /___ /___

| Description | Amount |
|---|---|
|  |  |
|  |  |
|  |  |
|  |  |
| Total |  |

Budget:

Brought forward:

# Weekly Expense Tracker

## Friday  Date ___ /___ /___

| Description | Amount |
|---|---|
|  |  |
|  |  |
|  |  |
|  |  |
|  |  |
|  |  |
| Total |  |

## Saturday  Date ___ /___ /___

| Description | Amount |
|---|---|
|  |  |
|  |  |
|  |  |
|  |  |
|  |  |
|  |  |
| Total |  |

## Sunday Date ___ /___ /___

| Description | Amount |
|---|---|
|  |  |
|  |  |
|  |  |
|  |  |
|  |  |
|  |  |
| Total |  |

## Notes

|  |
|---|
|  |
|  |
|  |
|  |
|  |
|  |
|  |

Budget:

Brought forward:

# Monthly Budget

## Income

| | |
|---|---|
| Income 1 | |
| Income 2 | |
| Other Income | |
| Total Income | |

## Expenses

Month

Budget

| Bill to be paid | Date due | Amount | Paid | Notes |
|---|---|---|---|---|
| | | | | |
| | | | | |
| | | | | |
| | | | | |
| | | | | |
| | | | | |
| | | | | |
| | | | | |
| | | | | |
| | | | | |
| | | | | |

# Other expenses

| Other Expenses | Date | Amount | Paid | Notes |
|---|---|---|---|---|
| | | | | |
| | | | | |
| | | | | |
| | | | | |
| | | | | |
| | | | | |
| | | | | |
| | | | | |
| | | | | |
| | | | | |
| Total | | | | |

Notes:

_____

_____

_____

_____

_____

# Weekly Expense Tracker

## Monday    Date ___ /___ /___

| Description | Amount |
|---|---|
|  |  |
|  |  |
|  |  |
|  |  |
|  |  |
| Total |  |

## Tuesday    Date ___ /___ /___

| Description | Amount |
|---|---|
|  |  |
|  |  |
|  |  |
|  |  |
|  |  |
| Total |  |

## Wednesday    Date ___ /___ /___

| Description | Amount |
|---|---|
|  |  |
|  |  |
|  |  |
|  |  |
|  |  |
| Total |  |

## Thursday    Date ___ /___ /___

| Description | Amount |
|---|---|
|  |  |
|  |  |
|  |  |
|  |  |
|  |  |
| Total |  |

Budget:

Brought forward:

# Weekly Expense Tracker

## Friday    Date ___ /___ /___

| Description | Amount |
|---|---|
|  |  |
|  |  |
|  |  |
|  |  |
|  |  |
|  |  |
| Total |  |

## Saturday    Date ___ /___ /___

| Description | Amount |
|---|---|
|  |  |
|  |  |
|  |  |
|  |  |
|  |  |
|  |  |
| Total |  |

## Sunday Date ___ /___ /___

| Description | Amount |
|---|---|
|  |  |
|  |  |
|  |  |
|  |  |
|  |  |
| Total |  |

## Notes

|  |
|---|
|  |
|  |
|  |
|  |
|  |
|  |
|  |

Budget:

Brought forward:

# Weekly Expense Tracker

## Monday    Date ___ /___ /___

| Description | Amount |
|---|---|
|  |  |
|  |  |
|  |  |
|  |  |
|  |  |
|  |  |
| Total |  |

## Tuesday    Date ___ /___ /___

| Description | Amount |
|---|---|
|  |  |
|  |  |
|  |  |
|  |  |
|  |  |
|  |  |
| Total |  |

## Wednesday   Date ___ /___ /___

| Description | Amount |
|---|---|
|  |  |
|  |  |
|  |  |
|  |  |
|  |  |
|  |  |
| Total |  |

## Thursday   Date ___ /___ /___

| Description | Amount |
|---|---|
|  |  |
|  |  |
|  |  |
|  |  |
|  |  |
| Total |  |

Budget:

Brought forward:

# Weekly Expense Tracker

## Friday   Date ___ /___ /___

| Description | Amount |
|---|---|
|  |  |
|  |  |
|  |  |
|  |  |
|  |  |
|  |  |
| Total |  |

## Saturday   Date ___ /___ /___

| Description | Amount |
|---|---|
|  |  |
|  |  |
|  |  |
|  |  |
|  |  |
|  |  |
| Total |  |

## Sunday Date ___ /___ /___

| Description | Amount |
|---|---|
|  |  |
|  |  |
|  |  |
|  |  |
|  |  |
|  |  |
| Total |  |

## Notes

|  |
|---|
|  |
|  |
|  |
|  |
|  |
|  |

Budget:

Brought forward:

# Weekly Expense Tracker

## Monday    Date ___ /___ /___

| Description | Amount |
|---|---|
|  |  |
|  |  |
|  |  |
|  |  |
|  |  |
| Total |  |

## Tuesday    Date ___ /___ /___

| Description | Amount |
|---|---|
|  |  |
|  |  |
|  |  |
|  |  |
|  |  |
| Total |  |

## Wednesday Date ___ /___ /___

| Description | Amount |
|---|---|
|  |  |
|  |  |
|  |  |
|  |  |
|  |  |
| Total |  |

## Thursday Date ___ /___ /___

| Description | Amount |
|---|---|
|  |  |
|  |  |
|  |  |
|  |  |
| Total |  |

Budget:

Brought forward:

# Weekly Expense Tracker

## Friday    Date ___ /___ /___

| Description | Amount |
|---|---|
|  |  |
|  |  |
|  |  |
|  |  |
|  |  |
|  |  |
| Total |  |

## Saturday    Date ___ /___ /___

| Description | Amount |
|---|---|
|  |  |
|  |  |
|  |  |
|  |  |
|  |  |
|  |  |
| Total |  |

## Sunday    Date ___ /___ /___

| Description | Amount |
|---|---|
|  |  |
|  |  |
|  |  |
|  |  |
|  |  |
| Total |  |

## Notes

Budget:

Brought Forward:

# Weekly Expense Tracker

## Monday    Date ___ / ___ / ___

| Description | Amount |
|---|---|
|  |  |
|  |  |
|  |  |
|  |  |
|  |  |
|  |  |
| Total |  |

## Tuesday    Date ___ / ___ / ___

| Description | Amount |
|---|---|
|  |  |
|  |  |
|  |  |
|  |  |
|  |  |
|  |  |
| Total |  |

## Wednesday Date ___ / ___ / ___

| Description | Amount |
|---|---|
|  |  |
|  |  |
|  |  |
|  |  |
|  |  |
|  |  |
| Total |  |

## Thursday Date ___ / ___ / ___

| Description | Amount |
|---|---|
|  |  |
|  |  |
|  |  |
|  |  |
|  |  |
| Total |  |

Budget:

Brought forward:

# Weekly Expense Tracker

## Friday   Date ___ /___ /___

| Description | Amount |
|---|---|
|  |  |
|  |  |
|  |  |
|  |  |
|  |  |
|  |  |
| Total |  |

## Saturday   Date ___ /___ /___

| Description | Amount |
|---|---|
|  |  |
|  |  |
|  |  |
|  |  |
|  |  |
|  |  |
| Total |  |

## Sunday   Date ___ /___ /___

| Description | Amount |
|---|---|
|  |  |
|  |  |
|  |  |
|  |  |
|  |  |
|  |  |
| Total |  |

## Notes

|  |
|---|
|  |
|  |
|  |
|  |
|  |
|  |

Budget:

Brought forward:

# Weekly Expense Tracker

## Monday    Date ___ /___ /___

| Description | Amount |
|---|---|
|  |  |
|  |  |
|  |  |
|  |  |
|  |  |
| Total |  |

## Tuesday    Date ___ /___ /___

| Description | Amount |
|---|---|
|  |  |
|  |  |
|  |  |
|  |  |
|  |  |
| Total |  |

## Wednesday    Date ___ /___ /___

| Description | Amount |
|---|---|
|  |  |
|  |  |
|  |  |
|  |  |
|  |  |
| Total |  |

## Thursday    Date ___ /___ /___

| Description | Amount |
|---|---|
|  |  |
|  |  |
|  |  |
|  |  |
| Total |  |

Budget:

Brought forward:

# Weekly Expense Tracker

## Friday    Date ___ /___ /___

| Description | Amount |
|---|---|
|  |  |
|  |  |
|  |  |
|  |  |
|  |  |
|  |  |
| Total |  |

## Saturday    Date ___ /___ /___

| Description | Amount |
|---|---|
|  |  |
|  |  |
|  |  |
|  |  |
|  |  |
|  |  |
| Total |  |

## Sunday  Date ___ /___ /___

| Description | Amount |
|---|---|
|  |  |
|  |  |
|  |  |
|  |  |
|  |  |
| Total |  |

## Notes

| |
|---|
|  |
|  |
|  |
|  |
|  |
|  |

Budget:

Brought forward:

# Monthly Budget

## Income

| | |
|---|---|
| Income 1 | |
| Income 2 | |
| Other Income | |
| Total Income | |

## Expenses

Month

Budget

| Bill to be paid | Date due | Amount | Paid | Notes |
|---|---|---|---|---|
| | | | | |
| | | | | |
| | | | | |
| | | | | |
| | | | | |
| | | | | |
| | | | | |
| | | | | |
| | | | | |
| | | | | |
| | | | | |

# Other expenses

| Other Expenses | Date | Amount | Paid | Notes |
|---|---|---|---|---|
|  |  |  |  |  |
|  |  |  |  |  |
|  |  |  |  |  |
|  |  |  |  |  |
|  |  |  |  |  |
|  |  |  |  |  |
|  |  |  |  |  |
|  |  |  |  |  |
|  |  |  |  |  |
|  |  |  |  |  |
| Total |  |  |  |  |

*Notes:*

_____

_____

_____

_____

# Weekly Expense Tracker

## Monday     Date ___ /___ /___

| Description | Amount |
|---|---|
|  |  |
|  |  |
|  |  |
|  |  |
|  |  |
| Total |  |

## Tuesday     Date ___ /___ /___

| Description | Amount |
|---|---|
|  |  |
|  |  |
|  |  |
|  |  |
|  |  |
| Total |  |

## Wednesday Date ___ /___ /___

| Description | Amount |
|---|---|
|  |  |
|  |  |
|  |  |
|  |  |
|  |  |
| Total |  |

## Thursday Date ___ /___ /___

| Description | Amount |
|---|---|
|  |  |
|  |  |
|  |  |
|  |  |
| Total |  |

Budget:

Brought forward:

# Weekly Expense Tracker

## Friday  Date ___ /___ /___

| Description | Amount |
|---|---|
|  |  |
|  |  |
|  |  |
|  |  |
|  |  |
|  |  |
| Total |  |

## Saturday  Date ___ /___ /___

| Description | Amount |
|---|---|
|  |  |
|  |  |
|  |  |
|  |  |
|  |  |
|  |  |
| Total |  |

## Sunday  Date ___ /___ /___

| Description | Amount |
|---|---|
|  |  |
|  |  |
|  |  |
|  |  |
|  |  |
|  |  |
| Total |  |

## Notes

| |
|---|
|  |
|  |
|  |
|  |
|  |
|  |
|  |

Budget:

Brought forward:

# Weekly Expense Tracker

## Monday    Date ___ /___ /___

| Description | Amount |
|---|---|
|  |  |
|  |  |
|  |  |
|  |  |
|  |  |
|  |  |
| Total |  |

## Tuesday    Date ___ /___ /___

| Description | Amount |
|---|---|
|  |  |
|  |  |
|  |  |
|  |  |
|  |  |
|  |  |
| Total |  |

## Wednesday    Date ___ /___ /___

| Description | Amount |
|---|---|
|  |  |
|  |  |
|  |  |
|  |  |
|  |  |
|  |  |
| Total |  |

## Thursday    Date ___ /___ /___

| Description | Amount |
|---|---|
|  |  |
|  |  |
|  |  |
|  |  |
|  |  |
| Total |  |

Budget:

Brought forward:

# Weekly Expense Tracker

## Friday  Date ___ /___ /___

| Description | Amount |
|---|---|
| | |
| | |
| | |
| | |
| | |
| | |
| Total | |

## Saturday  Date ___ /___ /___

| Description | Amount |
|---|---|
| | |
| | |
| | |
| | |
| | |
| | |
| Total | |

## Sunday Date ___ /___ /___

| Description | Amount |
|---|---|
| | |
| | |
| | |
| | |
| | |
| Total | |

## Notes

| |
|---|
| |
| |
| |
| |
| |
| |

Budget:

Brought forward:

# Weekly Expense Tracker

## Monday    Date ___ /___ /___

| Description | Amount |
|---|---|
|  |  |
|  |  |
|  |  |
|  |  |
|  |  |
| Total |  |

## Tuesday    Date ___ /___ /___

| Description | Amount |
|---|---|
|  |  |
|  |  |
|  |  |
|  |  |
|  |  |
| Total |  |

## Wednesday Date ___ /___ /___

| Description | Amount |
|---|---|
|  |  |
|  |  |
|  |  |
|  |  |
|  |  |
| Total |  |

## Thursday Date ___ /___ /___

| Description | Amount |
|---|---|
|  |  |
|  |  |
|  |  |
|  |  |
| Total |  |

Budget:

Brought forward:

# Weekly Expense Tracker

## Friday   Date ___ /___ /___

| Description | Amount |
|---|---|
|  |  |
|  |  |
|  |  |
|  |  |
|  |  |
|  |  |
| Total |  |

## Saturday   Date ___ /___ /___

| Description | Amount |
|---|---|
|  |  |
|  |  |
|  |  |
|  |  |
|  |  |
|  |  |
| Total |  |

## Sunday Date ___ /___ /___

| Description | Amount |
|---|---|
|  |  |
|  |  |
|  |  |
|  |  |
|  |  |
|  |  |
| Total |  |

## Notes

|  |
|---|
|  |
|  |
|  |
|  |
|  |
|  |
|  |

Budget:

Brought forward:

# Weekly Expense Tracker

## Monday    Date ___ /___ /___

| Description | Amount |
|---|---|
|  |  |
|  |  |
|  |  |
|  |  |
|  |  |
| Total |  |

## Tuesday    Date ___ /___ /___

| Description | Amount |
|---|---|
|  |  |
|  |  |
|  |  |
|  |  |
|  |  |
| Total |  |

## Wednesday    Date ___ /___ /___

| Description | Amount |
|---|---|
|  |  |
|  |  |
|  |  |
|  |  |
|  |  |
| Total |  |

## Thursday    Date ___ /___ /___

| Description | Amount |
|---|---|
|  |  |
|  |  |
|  |  |
|  |  |
|  |  |
| Total |  |

Budget:

Brought forward:

# Weekly Expense Tracker

## Friday    Date ___ /___ /___

| Description | Amount |
|---|---|
|  |  |
|  |  |
|  |  |
|  |  |
|  |  |
| Total |  |

## Saturday    Date ___ /___ /___

| Description | Amount |
|---|---|
|  |  |
|  |  |
|  |  |
|  |  |
| Total |  |

## Sunday    Date ___ /___ /___

| Description | Amount |
|---|---|
|  |  |
|  |  |
|  |  |
|  |  |
|  |  |
| Total |  |

## Notes

|  |
|---|
|  |
|  |
|  |
|  |
|  |

Budget:

Brought forward:

# Weekly Expense Tracker

## Monday   Date ___ /___ /___

| Description | Amount |
|---|---|
|  |  |
|  |  |
|  |  |
|  |  |
|  |  |
|  |  |
| Total |  |

## Tuesday   Date ___ /___ /___

| Description | Amount |
|---|---|
|  |  |
|  |  |
|  |  |
|  |  |
|  |  |
|  |  |
| Total |  |

## Wednesday   Date ___ /___ /___

| Description | Amount |
|---|---|
|  |  |
|  |  |
|  |  |
|  |  |
|  |  |
|  |  |
| Total |  |

## Thursday   Date ___ /___ /___

| Description | Amount |
|---|---|
|  |  |
|  |  |
|  |  |
|  |  |
|  |  |
| Total |  |

Budget:

Brought forward:

# Weekly Expense Tracker

## Friday    Date ___ / ___ / ___

| Description | Amount |
|---|---|
|  |  |
|  |  |
|  |  |
|  |  |
|  |  |
|  |  |
| Total |  |

## Saturday    Date ___ / ___ / ___

| Description | Amount |
|---|---|
|  |  |
|  |  |
|  |  |
|  |  |
|  |  |
|  |  |
| Total |  |

## Sunday    Date ___ / ___ / ___

| Description | Amount |
|---|---|
|  |  |
|  |  |
|  |  |
|  |  |
|  |  |
| Total |  |

## Notes

|  |
|---|
|  |
|  |
|  |
|  |
|  |
|  |

Budget:

Brought forward:

# Monthly Budget

## Income

| | |
|---|---|
| Income 1 | |
| Income 2 | |
| Other Income | |
| Total Income | |

## Expenses

Month

Budget

| Bill to be paid | Date due | Amount | Paid | Notes |
|---|---|---|---|---|
| | | | | |
| | | | | |
| | | | | |
| | | | | |
| | | | | |
| | | | | |
| | | | | |
| | | | | |
| | | | | |
| | | | | |
| | | | | |

# Other expenses

| Other Expenses | Date | Amount | Paid | Notes |
|---|---|---|---|---|
|  |  |  |  |  |
|  |  |  |  |  |
|  |  |  |  |  |
|  |  |  |  |  |
|  |  |  |  |  |
|  |  |  |  |  |
|  |  |  |  |  |
|  |  |  |  |  |
|  |  |  |  |  |
|  |  |  |  |  |
| Total |  |  |  |  |

## Notes:

# Weekly Expense Tracker

## Monday   Date ___ /___ /___

| Description | Amount |
|---|---|
| | |
| | |
| | |
| | |
| | |
| Total | |

## Tuesday   Date ___ /___ /___

| Description | Amount |
|---|---|
| | |
| | |
| | |
| | |
| | |
| Total | |

## Wednesday   Date ___ /___ /___

| Description | Amount |
|---|---|
| | |
| | |
| | |
| | |
| | |
| Total | |

## Thursday   Date ___ /___ /___

| Description | Amount |
|---|---|
| | |
| | |
| | |
| | |
| | |
| Total | |

Budget:

Brought forward:

# Weekly Expense Tracker

## Friday     Date ___ /___ /___

| Description | Amount |
|-------------|--------|
|             |        |
|             |        |
|             |        |
|             |        |
|             |        |
|             |        |
| Total       |        |

## Saturday     Date ___ /___ /___

| Description | Amount |
|-------------|--------|
|             |        |
|             |        |
|             |        |
|             |        |
|             |        |
|             |        |
| Total       |        |

## Sunday   Date ___ /___ /___

| Description | Amount |
|-------------|--------|
|             |        |
|             |        |
|             |        |
|             |        |
|             |        |
| Total       |        |

## Notes

|   |
|---|
|   |
|   |
|   |
|   |
|   |
|   |

Budget:

Brought forward:

# Weekly Expense Tracker

## Monday    Date ___ / ___ / ___

| Description | Amount |
|---|---|
|  |  |
|  |  |
|  |  |
|  |  |
|  |  |
| Total |  |

## Tuesday    Date ___ / ___ / ___

| Description | Amount |
|---|---|
|  |  |
|  |  |
|  |  |
|  |  |
|  |  |
| Total |  |

## Wednesday Date ___ / ___ / ___

| Description | Amount |
|---|---|
|  |  |
|  |  |
|  |  |
|  |  |
|  |  |
| Total |  |

## Thursday Date ___ / ___ / ___

| Description | Amount |
|---|---|
|  |  |
|  |  |
|  |  |
|  |  |
| Total |  |

Budget:

Brought forward:

# Weekly Expense Tracker

## Friday   Date ___ /___ /___

| Description | Amount |
|---|---|
|  |  |
|  |  |
|  |  |
|  |  |
|  |  |
| Total |  |

## Saturday   Date ___ /___ /___

| Description | Amount |
|---|---|
|  |  |
|  |  |
|  |  |
|  |  |
|  |  |
| Total |  |

## Sunday   Date ___ /___ /___

| Description | Amount |
|---|---|
|  |  |
|  |  |
|  |  |
|  |  |
|  |  |
| Total |  |

## Notes

|  |
|---|
|  |
|  |
|  |
|  |
|  |
|  |

Budget:

Brought forward:

# Weekly Expense Tracker

## Monday   Date ___ /___ /___

| Description | Amount |
|---|---|
|  |  |
|  |  |
|  |  |
|  |  |
|  |  |
|  |  |
| Total |  |

## Tuesday   Date ___ /___ /___

| Description | Amount |
|---|---|
|  |  |
|  |  |
|  |  |
|  |  |
|  |  |
|  |  |
| Total |  |

## Wednesday   Date ___ /___ /___

| Description | Amount |
|---|---|
|  |  |
|  |  |
|  |  |
|  |  |
|  |  |
| Total |  |

## Thursday   Date ___ /___ /___

| Description | Amount |
|---|---|
|  |  |
|  |  |
|  |  |
|  |  |
|  |  |
| Total |  |

Budget:

Brought forward:

# Weekly Expense Tracker

## Friday  Date ___ /___ /___

| Description | Amount |
|---|---|
|  |  |
|  |  |
|  |  |
|  |  |
|  |  |
|  |  |
| Total |  |

## Saturday  Date ___ /___ /___

| Description | Amount |
|---|---|
|  |  |
|  |  |
|  |  |
|  |  |
|  |  |
|  |  |
| Total |  |

## Sunday Date ___ /___ /___

| Description | Amount |
|---|---|
|  |  |
|  |  |
|  |  |
|  |  |
|  |  |
| Total |  |

## Notes

|  |
|---|
|  |
|  |
|  |
|  |
|  |
|  |

Budget:

Brought forward:

# Weekly Expense Tracker

## Monday    Date ___ /___ /___

| Description | Amount |
|---|---|
|  |  |
|  |  |
|  |  |
|  |  |
|  |  |
| Total |  |

## Tuesday    Date ___ /___ /___

| Description | Amount |
|---|---|
|  |  |
|  |  |
|  |  |
|  |  |
|  |  |
| Total |  |

## Wednesday   Date ___ /___ /___

| Description | Amount |
|---|---|
|  |  |
|  |  |
|  |  |
|  |  |
|  |  |
| Total |  |

## Thursday   Date ___ /___ /___

| Description | Amount |
|---|---|
|  |  |
|  |  |
|  |  |
|  |  |
|  |  |
| Total |  |

Budget:

Brought forward:

# Weekly Expense Tracker

## Friday   Date ___ /___ /___

| Description | Amount |
|-------------|--------|
|             |        |
|             |        |
|             |        |
|             |        |
|             |        |
|             |        |
| Total       |        |

## Saturday   Date ___ /___ /___

| Description | Amount |
|-------------|--------|
|             |        |
|             |        |
|             |        |
|             |        |
|             |        |
|             |        |
| Total       |        |

## Sunday   Date ___ /___ /___

| Description | Amount |
|-------------|--------|
|             |        |
|             |        |
|             |        |
|             |        |
|             |        |
| Total       |        |

## Notes

Budget:

Brought forward:

# Weekly Expense Tracker

## Monday    Date ___ /___ /___

| Description | Amount |
|---|---|
| | |
| | |
| | |
| | |
| | |
| | |
| Total | |

## Tuesday    Date ___ /___ /___

| Description | Amount |
|---|---|
| | |
| | |
| | |
| | |
| | |
| | |
| Total | |

## Wednesday    Date ___ /___ /___

| Description | Amount |
|---|---|
| | |
| | |
| | |
| | |
| | |
| | |
| Total | |

## Thursday    Date ___ /___ /___

| Description | Amount |
|---|---|
| | |
| | |
| | |
| | |
| | |
| Total | |

Budget:

Brought forward:

# Weekly Expense Tracker

## Friday   Date ___ /___ /___

| Description | Amount |
|---|---|
|  |  |
|  |  |
|  |  |
|  |  |
|  |  |
|  |  |
| Total |  |

## Saturday   Date ___ /___ /___

| Description | Amount |
|---|---|
|  |  |
|  |  |
|  |  |
|  |  |
|  |  |
|  |  |
| Total |  |

## Sunday   Date ___ /___ /___

| Description | Amount |
|---|---|
|  |  |
|  |  |
|  |  |
|  |  |
|  |  |
| Total |  |

## Notes

|  |
|---|
|  |
|  |
|  |
|  |
|  |
|  |

Budget:

Brought forward:

# Monthly Budget

## Income

| | |
|---|---|
| Income 1 | |
| Income 2 | |
| Other Income | |
| Total Income | |

## Expenses

Month

Budget

| Bill to be paid | Date due | Amount | Paid | Notes |
|---|---|---|---|---|
| | | | | |
| | | | | |
| | | | | |
| | | | | |
| | | | | |
| | | | | |
| | | | | |
| | | | | |
| | | | | |
| | | | | |
| | | | | |

# Other expenses

| other Expenses | Date | Amount | Paid | Notes |
|----------------|------|--------|------|-------|
|                |      |        |      |       |
|                |      |        |      |       |
|                |      |        |      |       |
|                |      |        |      |       |
|                |      |        |      |       |
|                |      |        |      |       |
|                |      |        |      |       |
|                |      |        |      |       |
|                |      |        |      |       |
|                |      |        |      |       |
| Total          |      |        |      |       |

Notes:

# Weekly Expense Tracker

## Monday     Date ___ / ___ / ___

| Description | Amount |
|---|---|
|  |  |
|  |  |
|  |  |
|  |  |
|  |  |
| Total |  |

## Tuesday     Date ___ / ___ / ___

| Description | Amount |
|---|---|
|  |  |
|  |  |
|  |  |
|  |  |
|  |  |
| Total |  |

## Wednesday Date ___ / ___ / ___

| Description | Amount |
|---|---|
|  |  |
|  |  |
|  |  |
|  |  |
|  |  |
| Total |  |

## Thursday Date ___ / ___ / ___

| Description | Amount |
|---|---|
|  |  |
|  |  |
|  |  |
|  |  |
|  |  |
| Total |  |

Budget:

Brought forward:

# Weekly Expense Tracker

## Friday   Date ___ /___ /___

| Description | Amount |
|---|---|
| | |
| | |
| | |
| | |
| | |
| Total | |

## Saturday   Date ___ /___ /___

| Description | Amount |
|---|---|
| | |
| | |
| | |
| | |
| | |
| Total | |

## Sunday   Date ___ /___ /___

| Description | Amount |
|---|---|
| | |
| | |
| | |
| | |
| | |
| Total | |

## Notes

| |
|---|
| |
| |
| |
| |
| |
| |

Budget:

Brought forward:

# Weekly Expense Tracker

## Monday    Date ___ /___ /___

| Description | Amount |
|---|---|
|  |  |
|  |  |
|  |  |
|  |  |
|  |  |
| Total |  |

## Tuesday    Date ___ /___ /___

| Description | Amount |
|---|---|
|  |  |
|  |  |
|  |  |
|  |  |
|  |  |
| Total |  |

## Wednesday Date ___ /___ /___

| Description | Amount |
|---|---|
|  |  |
|  |  |
|  |  |
|  |  |
|  |  |
| Total |  |

## Thursday Date ___ /___ /___

| Description | Amount |
|---|---|
|  |  |
|  |  |
|  |  |
|  |  |
|  |  |
| Total |  |

Budget:                    Brought forward:

# Weekly Expense Tracker

## Friday   Date ___ /___ /___

| Description | Amount |
|---|---|
|  |  |
|  |  |
|  |  |
|  |  |
|  |  |
|  |  |
| Total |  |

## Saturday   Date ___ /___ /___

| Description | Amount |
|---|---|
|  |  |
|  |  |
|  |  |
|  |  |
|  |  |
|  |  |
| Total |  |

## Sunday Date ___ /___ /___

| Description | Amount |
|---|---|
|  |  |
|  |  |
|  |  |
|  |  |
|  |  |
| Total |  |

## Notes

|  |
|---|
|  |
|  |
|  |
|  |
|  |
|  |

Budget:

Brought forward:

# Weekly Expense Tracker

## Monday    Date ___ /___ /___

| Description | Amount |
|---|---|
|  |  |
|  |  |
|  |  |
|  |  |
|  |  |
|  |  |
| Total |  |

## Tuesday    Date ___ /___ /___

| Description | Amount |
|---|---|
|  |  |
|  |  |
|  |  |
|  |  |
|  |  |
|  |  |
| Total |  |

## Wednesday  Date ___ /___ /___

| Description | Amount |
|---|---|
|  |  |
|  |  |
|  |  |
|  |  |
|  |  |
|  |  |
| Total |  |

## Thursday  Date ___ /___ /___

| Description | Amount |
|---|---|
|  |  |
|  |  |
|  |  |
|  |  |
|  |  |
|  |  |
| Total |  |

Budget:

Brought forward:

# Weekly Expense Tracker

## Friday    Date ___ /___ /___

| Description | Amount |
|---|---|
| | |
| | |
| | |
| | |
| | |
| | |
| Total | |

## Saturday    Date ___ /___ /___

| Description | Amount |
|---|---|
| | |
| | |
| | |
| | |
| | |
| | |
| Total | |

## Sunday    Date ___ /___ /___

| Description | Amount |
|---|---|
| | |
| | |
| | |
| | |
| | |
| Total | |

## Notes

Budget:

Brought forward:

# Weekly Expense Tracker

## Monday    Date ___ / ___ / ___

| Description | Amount |
|---|---|
|  |  |
|  |  |
|  |  |
|  |  |
|  |  |
|  |  |
| Total |  |

## Tuesday    Date ___ / ___ / ___

| Description | Amount |
|---|---|
|  |  |
|  |  |
|  |  |
|  |  |
|  |  |
|  |  |
| Total |  |

## Wednesday    Date ___ / ___ / ___

| Description | Amount |
|---|---|
|  |  |
|  |  |
|  |  |
|  |  |
|  |  |
|  |  |
| Total |  |

## Thursday    Date ___ / ___ / ___

| Description | Amount |
|---|---|
|  |  |
|  |  |
|  |  |
|  |  |
|  |  |
| Total |  |

Budget:

Brought forward:

# Weekly Expense Tracker

## Friday    Date ___ /___ /___

| Description | Amount |
|---|---|
|  |  |
|  |  |
|  |  |
|  |  |
|  |  |
|  |  |
| Total |  |

## Saturday    Date ___ /___ /___

| Description | Amount |
|---|---|
|  |  |
|  |  |
|  |  |
|  |  |
|  |  |
|  |  |
| Total |  |

## Sunday    Date ___ /___ /___

| Description | Amount |
|---|---|
|  |  |
|  |  |
|  |  |
|  |  |
|  |  |
| Total |  |

## Notes

|  |
|---|
|  |
|  |
|  |
|  |
|  |
|  |

Budget:

Brought forward:

# Weekly Expense Tracker

## Monday    Date ___/___/___

| Description | Amount |
|---|---|
|  |  |
|  |  |
|  |  |
|  |  |
|  |  |
| Total |  |

## Tuesday    Date ___/___/___

| Description | Amount |
|---|---|
|  |  |
|  |  |
|  |  |
|  |  |
|  |  |
| Total |  |

## Wednesday Date ___/___/___

| Description | Amount |
|---|---|
|  |  |
|  |  |
|  |  |
|  |  |
|  |  |
| Total |  |

## Thursday Date ___/___/___

| Description | Amount |
|---|---|
|  |  |
|  |  |
|  |  |
|  |  |
| Total |  |

Budget:

Brought forward:

# Weekly Expense Tracker

## Friday  Date ___ /___ /___

| Description | Amount |
|---|---|
|  |  |
|  |  |
|  |  |
|  |  |
|  |  |
|  |  |
| Total |  |

## Saturday  Date ___ /___ /___

| Description | Amount |
|---|---|
|  |  |
|  |  |
|  |  |
|  |  |
|  |  |
|  |  |
| Total |  |

## Sunday  Date ___ /___ /___

| Description | Amount |
|---|---|
|  |  |
|  |  |
|  |  |
|  |  |
|  |  |
| Total |  |

## Notes

|  |
|---|
|  |
|  |
|  |
|  |
|  |
|  |

Budget:

Brought forward:

# Monthly Budget

## Income

| | |
|---|---|
| Income 1 | |
| Income 2 | |
| Other Income | |
| Total Income | |

## Expenses

Month

Budget

| Bill to be paid | Date due | Amount | Paid | Notes |
|---|---|---|---|---|
| | | | | |
| | | | | |
| | | | | |
| | | | | |
| | | | | |
| | | | | |
| | | | | |
| | | | | |
| | | | | |
| | | | | |
| | | | | |

# Other expenses

| other Expenses | Date | Amount | Paid | Notes |
|---|---|---|---|---|
| | | | | |
| | | | | |
| | | | | |
| | | | | |
| | | | | |
| | | | | |
| | | | | |
| | | | | |
| | | | | |
| | | | | |
| | | | | |
| Total | | | | |

*Notes:*

_____

_____

_____

_____

_____

# Weekly Expense Tracker

## Monday    Date ___ /___ /___

| Description | Amount |
|---|---|
|  |  |
|  |  |
|  |  |
|  |  |
|  |  |
| Total |  |

## Tuesday    Date ___ /___ /___

| Description | Amount |
|---|---|
|  |  |
|  |  |
|  |  |
|  |  |
|  |  |
| Total |  |

## Wednesday    Date ___ /___ /___

| Description | Amount |
|---|---|
|  |  |
|  |  |
|  |  |
|  |  |
|  |  |
| Total |  |

## Thursday    Date ___ /___ /___

| Description | Amount |
|---|---|
|  |  |
|  |  |
|  |  |
|  |  |
|  |  |
| Total |  |

Budget:

Brought forward:

# Weekly Expense Tracker

## Friday    Date ___ /___ /___

| Description | Amount |
|---|---|
|  |  |
|  |  |
|  |  |
|  |  |
|  |  |
| Total |  |

## Saturday    Date ___ /___ /___

| Description | Amount |
|---|---|
|  |  |
|  |  |
|  |  |
|  |  |
|  |  |
| Total |  |

## Sunday Date ___ /___ /___

| Description | Amount |
|---|---|
|  |  |
|  |  |
|  |  |
|  |  |
|  |  |
| Total |  |

## Notes

|  |
|---|
|  |
|  |
|  |
|  |
|  |

Budget:

Brought forward:

# Weekly Expense Tracker

## Monday    Date ___ /___ /___

| Description | Amount |
|---|---|
|  |  |
|  |  |
|  |  |
|  |  |
|  |  |
| Total |  |

## Tuesday    Date ___ /___ /___

| Description | Amount |
|---|---|
|  |  |
|  |  |
|  |  |
|  |  |
|  |  |
| Total |  |

## Wednesday Date ___ /___ /___

| Description | Amount |
|---|---|
|  |  |
|  |  |
|  |  |
|  |  |
|  |  |
| Total |  |

## Thursday Date ___ /___ /___

| Description | Amount |
|---|---|
|  |  |
|  |  |
|  |  |
|  |  |
| Total |  |

Budget:                    Brought forward:

# Weekly Expense Tracker

## Friday    Date ___ /___ /___

| Description | Amount |
|---|---|
|  |  |
|  |  |
|  |  |
|  |  |
|  |  |
|  |  |
| Total |  |

## Saturday    Date ___ /___ /___

| Description | Amount |
|---|---|
|  |  |
|  |  |
|  |  |
|  |  |
|  |  |
|  |  |
| Total |  |

## Sunday    Date ___ /___ /___

| Description | Amount |
|---|---|
|  |  |
|  |  |
|  |  |
|  |  |
|  |  |
|  |  |
| Total |  |

## Notes

Budget:

Brought forward:

# Weekly Expense Tracker

## Monday    Date ___ /___ /___

| Description | Amount |
|---|---|
|  |  |
|  |  |
|  |  |
|  |  |
|  |  |
| Total |  |

## Tuesday    Date ___ /___ /___

| Description | Amount |
|---|---|
|  |  |
|  |  |
|  |  |
|  |  |
|  |  |
| Total |  |

## Wednesday Date ___ /___ /___

| Description | Amount |
|---|---|
|  |  |
|  |  |
|  |  |
|  |  |
|  |  |
| Total |  |

## Thursday Date ___ /___ /___

| Description | Amount |
|---|---|
|  |  |
|  |  |
|  |  |
|  |  |
|  |  |
| Total |  |

Budget:

Brought forward:

# Weekly Expense Tracker

## Friday     Date ___ /___ /___

| Description | Amount |
|---|---|
|  |  |
|  |  |
|  |  |
|  |  |
|  |  |
| Total |  |

## Saturday     Date ___ /___ /___

| Description | Amount |
|---|---|
|  |  |
|  |  |
|  |  |
|  |  |
| Total |  |

## Sunday  Date ___ /___ /___

| Description | Amount |
|---|---|
|  |  |
|  |  |
|  |  |
|  |  |
|  |  |
| Total |  |

## Notes

|  |
|---|
|  |
|  |
|  |
|  |
|  |
|  |

Budget:

Brought forward:

# Weekly Expense Tracker

## Monday  Date ___ /___ /___

| Description | Amount |
|---|---|
|  |  |
|  |  |
|  |  |
|  |  |
|  |  |
| Total |  |

## Tuesday  Date ___ /___ /___

| Description | Amount |
|---|---|
|  |  |
|  |  |
|  |  |
|  |  |
|  |  |
| Total |  |

## Wednesday  Date ___ /___ /___

| Description | Amount |
|---|---|
|  |  |
|  |  |
|  |  |
|  |  |
|  |  |
| Total |  |

## Thursday  Date ___ /___ /___

| Description | Amount |
|---|---|
|  |  |
|  |  |
|  |  |
|  |  |
| Total |  |

Budget:

Brought forward:

# Weekly Expense Tracker

## Friday    Date ___ /___ /___

| Description | Amount |
|-------------|--------|
|             |        |
|             |        |
|             |        |
|             |        |
|             |        |
|             |        |
| Total       |        |

## Saturday    Date ___ /___ /___

| Description | Amount |
|-------------|--------|
|             |        |
|             |        |
|             |        |
|             |        |
|             |        |
|             |        |
| Total       |        |

## Sunday Date ___ /___ /___

| Description | Amount |
|-------------|--------|
|             |        |
|             |        |
|             |        |
|             |        |
|             |        |
| Total       |        |

## Notes

Budget:

Brought forward:

# Weekly Expense Tracker

## Monday  Date ___ /___ /___

| Description | Amount |
|---|---|
| | |
| | |
| | |
| | |
| | |
| | |
| Total | |

## Tuesday  Date ___ /___ /___

| Description | Amount |
|---|---|
| | |
| | |
| | |
| | |
| | |
| | |
| Total | |

## Wednesday Date ___ /___ /___

| Description | Amount |
|---|---|
| | |
| | |
| | |
| | |
| | |
| | |
| Total | |

## Thursday Date ___ /___ /___

| Description | Amount |
|---|---|
| | |
| | |
| | |
| | |
| | |
| Total | |

Budget:

Brought forward:

# Weekly Expense Tracker

## Friday  Date ___ /___ /___

| Description | Amount |
|---|---|
|  |  |
|  |  |
|  |  |
|  |  |
|  |  |
|  |  |
| Total |  |

## Saturday  Date ___ /___ /___

| Description | Amount |
|---|---|
|  |  |
|  |  |
|  |  |
|  |  |
|  |  |
|  |  |
| Total |  |

## Sunday  Date ___ /___ /___

| Description | Amount |
|---|---|
|  |  |
|  |  |
|  |  |
|  |  |
|  |  |
| Total |  |

## Notes

Budget:

Brought forward:

# Monthly Budget

## Income

| | |
|---|---|
| Income 1 | |
| Income 2 | |
| Other Income | |
| Total Income | |

## Expenses

Month

Budget

| Bill to be paid | Date due | Amount | Paid | Notes |
|---|---|---|---|---|
| | | | | |
| | | | | |
| | | | | |
| | | | | |
| | | | | |
| | | | | |
| | | | | |
| | | | | |
| | | | | |
| | | | | |
| | | | | |
| | | | | |

# Other expenses

| other Expenses | Date | Amount | Paid | Notes |
|---|---|---|---|---|
| | | | | |
| | | | | |
| | | | | |
| | | | | |
| | | | | |
| | | | | |
| | | | | |
| | | | | |
| | | | | |
| | | | | |
| | | | | |
| Total | | | | |

Notes:

_____
_____
_____
_____
_____

# Weekly Expense Tracker

## Monday  Date ___ /___ /___

| Description | Amount |
|---|---|
| | |
| | |
| | |
| | |
| | |
| | |
| Total | |

## Tuesday  Date ___ /___ /___

| Description | Amount |
|---|---|
| | |
| | |
| | |
| | |
| | |
| | |
| Total | |

## Wednesday  Date ___ /___ /___

| Description | Amount |
|---|---|
| | |
| | |
| | |
| | |
| | |
| | |
| Total | |

## Thursday  Date ___ /___ /___

| Description | Amount |
|---|---|
| | |
| | |
| | |
| | |
| | |
| Total | |

Budget:

Brought forward:

# Weekly Expense Tracker

## Friday Date ___ /___ /___

| Description | Amount |
|---|---|
|  |  |
|  |  |
|  |  |
|  |  |
|  |  |
|  |  |
| Total |  |

## Saturday Date ___ /___ /___

| Description | Amount |
|---|---|
|  |  |
|  |  |
|  |  |
|  |  |
|  |  |
|  |  |
| Total |  |

## Sunday Date ___ /___ /___

| Description | Amount |
|---|---|
|  |  |
|  |  |
|  |  |
|  |  |
|  |  |
| Total |  |

## Notes

Budget:

Brought forward:

# Weekly Expense Tracker

## Monday    Date ___ /___ /___

| Description | Amount |
|---|---|
|  |  |
|  |  |
|  |  |
|  |  |
|  |  |
| Total |  |

## Tuesday    Date ___ /___ /___

| Description | Amount |
|---|---|
|  |  |
|  |  |
|  |  |
|  |  |
|  |  |
| Total |  |

## Wednesday Date ___ /___ /___

| Description | Amount |
|---|---|
|  |  |
|  |  |
|  |  |
|  |  |
|  |  |
| Total |  |

## Thursday Date ___ /___ /___

| Description | Amount |
|---|---|
|  |  |
|  |  |
|  |  |
|  |  |
|  |  |
| Total |  |

Budget:

Brought forward:

# Weekly Expense Tracker

## Friday    Date ___ /___ /___

| Description | Amount |
|---|---|
| | |
| | |
| | |
| | |
| | |
| | |
| Total | |

## Saturday    Date ___ /___ /___

| Description | Amount |
|---|---|
| | |
| | |
| | |
| | |
| | |
| | |
| Total | |

## Sunday   Date ___ /___ /___

| Description | Amount |
|---|---|
| | |
| | |
| | |
| | |
| | |
| | |
| Total | |

## Notes

| |
|---|
| |
| |
| |
| |
| |
| |

Budget:

Brought forward:

# Weekly Expense Tracker

## Monday          Date ___ /___ /___

| Description | Amount |
|---|---|
|  |  |
|  |  |
|  |  |
|  |  |
|  |  |
| Total |  |

## Tuesday          Date ___ /___ /___

| Description | Amount |
|---|---|
|  |  |
|  |  |
|  |  |
|  |  |
|  |  |
| Total |  |

## Wednesday Date ___ /___ /___

| Description | Amount |
|---|---|
|  |  |
|  |  |
|  |  |
|  |  |
|  |  |
| Total |  |

## Thursday Date ___ /___ /___

| Description | Amount |
|---|---|
|  |  |
|  |  |
|  |  |
|  |  |
|  |  |
| Total |  |

Budget:

Brought forward:

# Weekly Expense Tracker

## Friday    Date ___ /___ /___

| Description | Amount |
|-------------|--------|
|  |  |
|  |  |
|  |  |
|  |  |
|  |  |
|  |  |
| Total |  |

## Saturday    Date ___ /___ /___

| Description | Amount |
|-------------|--------|
|  |  |
|  |  |
|  |  |
|  |  |
|  |  |
|  |  |
| Total |  |

## Sunday Date ___ /___ /___

| Description | Amount |
|-------------|--------|
|  |  |
|  |  |
|  |  |
|  |  |
|  |  |
| Total |  |

## Notes

| |
|---|
| |
| |
| |
| |
| |
| |

Budget:

Brought forward:

# Weekly Expense Tracker

## Monday   Date ___ /___ /___

| Description | Amount |
|---|---|
|  |  |
|  |  |
|  |  |
|  |  |
|  |  |
|  |  |
| Total |  |

## Tuesday   Date ___ /___ /___

| Description | Amount |
|---|---|
|  |  |
|  |  |
|  |  |
|  |  |
|  |  |
|  |  |
| Total |  |

## Wednesday   Date ___ /___ /___

| Description | Amount |
|---|---|
|  |  |
|  |  |
|  |  |
|  |  |
|  |  |
|  |  |
| Total |  |

## Thursday   Date ___ /___ /___

| Description | Amount |
|---|---|
|  |  |
|  |  |
|  |  |
|  |  |
|  |  |
| Total |  |

Budget:

Brought forward:

# Weekly Expense Tracker

## Friday Date ___ /___ /___

| Description | Amount |
|---|---|
| | |
| | |
| | |
| | |
| | |
| | |
| Total | |

## Saturday Date ___ /___ /___

| Description | Amount |
|---|---|
| | |
| | |
| | |
| | |
| | |
| | |
| Total | |

## Sunday Date ___ /___ /___

| Description | Amount |
|---|---|
| | |
| | |
| | |
| | |
| | |
| | |
| Total | |

## Notes

| |
|---|
| |
| |
| |
| |
| |
| |

Budget:

Brought forward:

# Weekly Expense Tracker

## Monday  Date ___ /___ /___

| Description | Amount |
|---|---|
|  |  |
|  |  |
|  |  |
|  |  |
|  |  |
|  |  |
| Total |  |

## Tuesday  Date ___ /___ /___

| Description | Amount |
|---|---|
|  |  |
|  |  |
|  |  |
|  |  |
|  |  |
|  |  |
| Total |  |

## Wednesday  Date ___ /___ /___

| Description | Amount |
|---|---|
|  |  |
|  |  |
|  |  |
|  |  |
|  |  |
|  |  |
| Total |  |

## Thursday  Date ___ /___ /___

| Description | Amount |
|---|---|
|  |  |
|  |  |
|  |  |
|  |  |
|  |  |
| Total |  |

Budget:

Brought forward:

# Weekly Expense Tracker

## Friday    Date ___ /___ /___

| Description | Amount |
|---|---|
|  |  |
|  |  |
|  |  |
|  |  |
|  |  |
| Total |  |

## Saturday    Date ___ /___ /___

| Description | Amount |
|---|---|
|  |  |
|  |  |
|  |  |
|  |  |
|  |  |
| Total |  |

## Sunday    Date ___ /___ /___

| Description | Amount |
|---|---|
|  |  |
|  |  |
|  |  |
|  |  |
|  |  |
| Total |  |

## Notes

|  |
|---|
|  |
|  |
|  |
|  |
|  |
|  |
|  |

Budget:

Brought forward:

# Notes

# Notes

# Notes

Made in the USA
Las Vegas, NV
14 August 2021